A Touch of Christmas Day

Written by
Dr Phillip & Meghan Deam

Foreword

Each year, as Christmas morning dawns, our family finds itself drawn together in the warm embrace of our family traditions. The laughter of our children as they rush down the hallway, the sparkle in their eyes as they discover the treasures left under the tree, and the warm hugs shared as we exchange gifts—these are the moments that make this season truly special.

This poem is a reflection of the joy we experience each year as we celebrate the Christmas as a family. It captures the essence of what Christmas means to us—a time to pause, to embrace, and to revel in the unfiltered happiness that this day brings. As you read through these verses, may you feel the warmth of our family's love and the magic of Christmas that fills our home.

Phillip Deam

The dawn breaks gently,

a small ray of light.

Signaling the end,

of this magical night.

The children awaken,

their eyes wide with delight.

Christmas morning has come,

their hearts taking flight.

Footsteps echo softly,

then quicken in pace.

Down the hallway they run,

with joy on each face.

Voices sing out,

their excitement fills the air.

"Mom, Dad, wake up!

Santa's been here."

In warm pajamas,

with laughter and cheer.

They run to the tree,

as presents appear.

The stockings are brimming,

the gifts piled high.

Under the twinkling lights,

a Christmas surprise.

Mom and Dad follow,

with smiles warm and bright.

Their hearts filled with love,

at this beautiful sight.

They sit with hot coffee,

in the glow of the tree,

As the children unwrap gifts,

their faces serene.

Each present revealed,

with wonder and joy.

The room is alive,

with the shouts of each girl and boy.

Moments like these,

are so precious and dear.

The true gifts of Christmas,

the ones we hold near.

Amongst the unwrapping,

the laughter, the play.

Our family feels the magic,

of this special day.

Family visits and hugs,

from those we don't see,

make the morning so special,

as we sit by the tree.

As it's not just the gifts,

the ribbons, the bows.

But the warmth of the family,

that truly bestows.

The magic of Christmas,

pure and divine.

A treasure for always,

this moment in time.

From our family to yours, we wish you a merry Christmas.

Phillip & Meghan Dean

www.ingramcontent.com/pod-product-compliance
Lightning Source LLC
Chambersburg PA
CBHW042359070526
44585CB00029B/2998